Reflections From a Teacher's Heart
The Affective Side of Middle Grades Education

by
David Puckett

National Middle School Association
Westerville, OH

National Middle School Association
4151 Executive Parkway, Suite 300
Westerville, Ohio 43081
Telephone (800) 528-NMSA

Second Printing, July 2002

Sue Swaim, Executive Director
Jeff Ward, Assistant Executive Director, Business
John Lounsbury, Consulting Editor, Professional Publications
Edward Brazee, Editor, Professional Publications
Mary Mitchell, Copy Editor/Designer
Marcia Meade-Hurst, Senior Publications Representative
Andrea Yost, Cover design

Library of Congress Cataloging-in-Publication Data
Puckett, David, date
    Reflections from a teacher's heart: the affective side of middle grades education/ by David Puckett.
        p. cm.
    ISBN: 1-56090-159-4 (pbk.)
    1. Middle school education--United States. 2. Affective education--United States.   I. Title
LB1623.5.P83   1999
373.236--dc21   99-11947
                                                        CIP

Foreword

David Puckett came to the realization over a period of years that while there was an abundance of "how to teach" books, there existed a dearth of materials on "how it *feels* to teach." He began writing free verse pieces at the end of a day's teaching in an effort to be a part of the solution rather than simply decrying the problem. His goal was "to reflect the full range of emotions experienced by all those lucky enough to call themselves middle grades teachers." The collection grew, and gradually others became aware of his work. They were impressed and encouraged him to share some of the verses in various meetings of fellow educators. When he did so, the positive responses were overwhelming. One such reader was M. Hayes Mizell of the Edna McConnell Clark Foundation. He suggested that David submit his work to National Middle School Association for consideration.

As a result, NMSA is pleased to make available to the profession and the public at large these insightful, engaging, sometimes serious, sometimes clever, often profound pieces. Readers will find them to be revealing representations of the nature of young adolescents and perceptive pictures of the distinctive qualities that make middle level teaching special.

Enjoy.

— JHL

About the Author

David Puckett teaches French and Social Studies at L.T. Johnson Traditional Middle School in Jefferson County, Kentucky. Now in his twentieth year of middle level teaching, he has often been recognized for professional excellence and service at local, state, and national levels. In 1995 he was selected as Jefferson County's Teacher of the Year. The following year he was the runner-up to Kentucky's Teacher of the Year. His team received first place, South Region, in the NMSA/Prentice Hall Teaching Team Awards in 1995. David contracted polio at age five and since 1992 has taught from his power wheelchair.

David Puckett received his A.B. degree at Eastern Kentucky University, M.Div. at Ashbury Theological Seminary, and M.A. Ed. from Western Kentucky University. He has been married for twenty-five years and has two children, now young adults.

Planning Period

Have you ever asked yourself,
"Why do they call a planning period,
A planning period?"
That precious 55 minutes each day is filled with...
Paper work,
Errands,
Parent conferences,
Extra duties,
Meetings,
Phone calls,
Gathering work for absentees...

I suppose that is precisely why they call it a planning period.
Simply because...
There's no time left for planning....
PERIOD!

Adolescents

I
do
see
them:
lively,
young,
growing
by leaps
and bounds;
bursting out
of poorly sewn,
mass-produced jeans,
to become individuals;
secure in their uniqueness;
no longer dependent on parents
or the uniformity of their own nonconformity:

castings dissatisfied with the constraints of the mold.

Middle school learning is...

gum hiding
pencil breaking
toe tapping
hair tossing
seat squirming
pocket searching
make-up checking
window watching
note writing
mind changing
note crumpling
allegiance shifting
girl dreaming
boy dreaming
day dreaming.

Middle school teaching is....

aiming the learning gun
at a moving target.

Somewhere
In the past of every successful human being
Stands a middle school teacher
with a
smoking gun.

Special Education

We lost another student today;
Second one this year.
First, Brian to a seizure in his sleep,
Now Scott, to a congenital heart defect.
I suppose you should expect problems,
When you deal with special needs children...
But you don't...
And you are never prepared for them.

I only saw those special kids during homeroom...
And at lunch...
And in the halls during the day,
When they would unabashedly and joyfully yell out,
"Hi, Mr. Puckett!"
Then, proudly say to their friends,
"That's my teacher!"

I only saw those special kids
Just enough
To learn to love them,
And to learn from them.

They've taught me their love of learning,
No matter how basic the lesson.

They've taught me the essence of acceptence...
That unconditional,
Unselfconscious,
Matter-of-fact,
"Here I am, whatcha gonna do about it?" attitude.

They've taught me to look forward to each day,
If for no other reason,
Because it has come.

They've taught me the reason they are known as
Special Education children:
Because that is precisely what they give us...
A special education
Not available from any graduate school in the land.

True Rewards

Marshall Sample
Regional Manager, Mechanical Engineering Firm
Fresh out of the university
$53,000 per year.

David Puckett
7th grade teacher, public school
159 students each day
17 years in the classroom
$37,000 per year.

Marshall was my student aide 10 years ago...
Tried hard...
Kept plugging.....
Wrote in scribbles...

Look at him now!

We had lunch today...
He paid.

Who says teaching doesn't have its rewards?

Thanks, Gloria

One of the best middle school counselors I have ever known,
Was not a counselor at all.
She was, however,
A wonderful listener,
Knew every child in the school by name,
Had a good word for each child every day,
Helped solve a multitude of crises,
And even knew what each child liked to eat!

But, when you think about it,
That's none too surprising.

She stood at the cafeteria cash register,
Day after day,
Counseling as she collected lunch money.

She's now cafeteria manager,
Doing trivial things like planning menus,
Ordering supplies,
Doing payroll,
Meeting federal and district guidelines.

Someone else has taken over her really important work.

The kids miss you, Gloria.

Daniel

You've gained weight, Daniel.
Not too much,
Just enough to lose that lanky,
Awkward look.

You've learned to smile,
Even laugh,
As you walk with your friends....
You never did that before.

You seem more confident,
More comfortable,
More self-assured.

What happened to that melancholy,
Thin,
Self-deprecating 14 year old,
Too wise for his years,
Who chose to sit alone for the first five months of school?

I realize your grades have gone from A's and B's
To B's and C's...
But, that's okay.
I'm thrilled to see you average and happy,
Rather than miserable and on the honor roll.

You'll never know how I've worried about you, Daniel.
Wondering if I had done the right thing...
Questioning my motives...
Doubting my own judgment.

Seeing you happy and alive
Is all I needed to let me know I was right
To call the Child Abuse Hotline.

Another Christmas

Another Christmas....
Another 17 coffee mugs....
Another 4 dozen chocolate chip cookies,
Slightly burned on the bottom by a child anxious to please....
Another collection of hard candies
in a full array of holiday colors....
All gaily wrapped,
Bowed,
and
Tagged.
Except for one.
Rolled tightly.
Bound by a single green ribbon....

A single sheet of typing paper.

John placed it on my desk,
Did not say a word,
And,
Sheepishly returned to his seat.

I completed taking attendance,
Got class started,
Explained our assignment,
And began a paperwork task of my own.
Then I remembered John's gift.

I fought back my emotions as I read the single page....
Thinking of John
Who
Could never stay in his seat...
Talked incessantly whether anyone was listening or not.
John,
Who, until recently,
Rarely completed his work.

I had exhausted myself with...
"John, sit down!"
"John, shhhh!"
"John, this isn't good enough. Please do it over!"
"John, I know you can do it!.....
I just wish you knew it too!"

With this page.....all the exhaustion evaporated
as I read.............

Dear Mr. Puckett,

    I want to tell you how I feel about you. I admire
two things about you. One is that you are a kind and
loving man. You try to comfort people when they are
unsure of themselves. For example, the time I was
unsure about me passing the math test and you told me,
"I want you not to let that bother you, and act like you
are the smartest kid on the team." I did that and I passed
the test, and that one small event has caused me to have
more self-esteem.
    Another thing I admire about you is your
strength, courage and persistence to keep teaching....
I believe that your faith has led you to this job, and
allowed you to keep teaching.
    I know you humble yourself, and you might
think you are just my teacher, but to me you are my
mentor. You have an undescribable feature I can't put my
finger on, and I know I have only known you for four
months, but I want to say thanks for everything.

        Sincerely,
        John Haveman

That single page
Taught me more
Than all those university courses.

That single page,
rolled tightly,
and wrapped with a single green ribbon,
Uplifted me as coffee mugs and hard candy will never do.

I dared not look up...
Knowing what would happen if I did.

I took an index card
From the stack on my desk
And wrote John a short note
Which said what I could not say aloud:

"John,
Thank you for the wonderful gift.
The truth is that YOU are the true gift.
You will never know how special you are!
Thank You,
Mr. P."

I passed, casually, by John's desk,
Slipped the note on it ,
And said nothing.
We carefully avoided eye contact,
But,
Later glanced up at the same instant
To catch a special moment in one another's memory.

Thanks to John...
And his letter...
Which now hangs, framed in my office,
Christmas will never be
"Just another Christmas."

Yes, Casey, Teaching Sometimes Tingles

We sat in the classroom,
Three minutes until dismissal.
Thirty one seventh graders...
One me.

As I looked out over the varying
Sizes,
And
Personalities,
And
Temperaments,
And
Natures,
I just had to tell them.
They deserved to know.

"Class",
I ventured tentatively,
"I will probably live to regret having said this....but...
I just love this group!
You are so much fun!
You have such neat personalities!
I don't know how to express it."

As usual,
The problem solves itself
When Casey pops up and asks,
"Do we make you tingle, Mr. P.?"

"Yes,"
I replied,
"That pretty well sums it up!"

Lessons From Experience
Shared With My Teaching Intern

Remember these general truths...

- Children glow when they are successful.
- Nothing breeds success, like success.
- When no one seems to be interested or listening, teach to the few who are, ...the rest will get caught up in the excitement.
- Talk to your students as though they were five years older than they really are; listen as though they were five years younger.
- Don't forget to water the plants before spring break!

Never...

- Try to get children to be quiet by being louder than they are.
- Read a sad story aloud in class, without having first read it to yourself.
- Assume the school supplies toilet tissue.
- Assume the kids have read the directions.
- Assume the kids understand the directions after they read them.
- Assume the cafeteria milk is fresh.
- Get a haircut in the middle of the week.
- Put your socks on in the dark.
- Say "No".......Say "Yes" in a way that equals "No."
- Forget to thank the lunchroom ladies.
- Go to school with a dryer sheet hanging from your sleeve.
- Let your teaching interfere with a child's education.

Remain calm when...

- Undergoing hormone-induced power surges.
- The classroom gerbil's babies are born in the middle of third period.
- Termites choose your classroom as a swarm site.

To break the monotony...

- Do short read-alouds.
- Rearrange the room.
- Seat children alphabetically by their middle names.
- Freshen the bulletin boards.
- Do curriculum-related jigsaw puzzles.
- Get laryngitis.
- Picture your most annoying student dressed as the opposite sex.
- Visualize your students 10...20...30 years from now.
- Visualize yourself 10...20...30 years ago.
- Compare your visions.
- Wear enormous "gag" sunglasses.
- Have your students study a topic YOU want to learn about.
- Be goofy.
- Teach all day, one whole day, as though you spoke the way Dr. Seuss writes.

According to a group of 150 students, a good teacher ALWAYS...

- Is nice.
- Listens to students.
- Asks how students are doing.
- Explains to students.
- Works with passion.
- Gives compliments.
- Rewards students.

- Is fair.
- Is firm.
- Loves students.
- Makes learning fun.
- Believes in students.
- Listens to both sides of a story.
- Gives candy (not the cheap stuff).
- Has fun teaching.
- Has time for students.
- Has an extra pencil.

**According to the same 150 students,
a good teacher NEVER..**

- Yells at students.
- Tells on students.
- Insults students.
- Embarrasses students.
- Singles out students in front of others.
- Picks favorites.
- Punishes all for one.
- Loses papers.
- Leaves the classroom.
- Gets angry.
- Assumes.
- Ignores a student.
- Gives up on students.

Testing Time

It's testing time again,
But something seems to bother me...
What am I really testing?
I mean REALLY!

Am I testing knowledge?
Memory?
Transferrance?
Application?
Ability to extend ideas?
Comfort with the stress of testing?

Or,
Am I simply taking a measure
Of the opportunity to learn that I have given a child?

Am I taking the pulse of a student's interest in learning?

Am I confirming the engagement factor...
Have my students truly been engaged in what we have spent
so much precious time studying?

Am I finding a correlation between learning and teaching?
Or
Am I expecting to find that learning has taken place in spite
of my teaching?

Yes,
It's testing time.
But... really...
Who am I truly testing?

The Middle School Workout

Neither Jane Fonda,
Nor Richard Simmons,
Could improve upon the daily workout
Performed by middle school students everywhere!

They are amazing!
Their rules are few...
Simple...
Universal:

1. Don't walk when you can run!
2. Don't whisper when you can yell!
3. If it's overhead, jump and hit it!
4. If it's underfoot, kick it!
5. If it's flat, wad it up and throw it!
6. If it's breathing, write a note to it!

No wonder their parents complain
That their children come home too tired
To do their homework!

The Middle Years

It's not easy...
Teaching the kids in the middle...
They're so headstrong,
They know it all.
They've forgotten how to walk.
They've remembered how to cry.
They're grown-up one day,
A child the next.
They hate the way they look.
They hate the way you look at them.
They hate their name.
They have little respect for anyone or anything.

They're hard.
They're hard to love...
They're hard to teach...
They're hard to understand...
They're hard.

Help me remember,
There's only one thing harder than
teaching the kid in the middle...

Being one!

17 Years in the Seventh Grade and I Still Haven't Learned

Four years of undergraduate work.
Two Master's degrees.
Seventeen years in the classroom.

I know concrete from abstract.
I can leap the tallest Bloom's Taxonomy in a single bound.
I actually do worry about Higher Order Thinking Skills.

I have mastered ...
content guidelines...
portfolio production...
writing process...
alternative assessment...
creating quality work!

And then comes Nick...
Perfect manners,
Well groomed,
The ideal student.

He's almost at my desk...
He probably has an insightful question...
He may have discovered an editing error in the new text.
He's such a good student.

What?
Let me see...

Nick stretches forth his hand...
And reminds me of what I all too often forget!

While I was focused on teaching ultimate truth,
Nick was pulling his last baby tooth.

When will I ever learn that I teach a "Who" not a "What!"

Ycanchube?

We had a conference with Mark's dad today.
Nice man.
Professional.
Articulate.
Concerned.
He had called for the conference.

We sat at the conference table in my classroom.
Five teachers...
Dad...
Mark...
To try to help Mark be more successful.

Dad says,
"What's going on with you, Mark?"
Mark shrugged.
"Ycanchube like your sister?"
Dad looks at us,
Says,
"His sister makes straight A's."
"Ycanchube like her, Mark?" he asks again.
Mark looks uncomfortable,
Doesn't reply.
"Ycanchu do your homework, Mark?
Your sister has homework every night.
Ycanchu pay attention, Mark?
You're not even listening now!"
Mark shrinks further down in his seat.

"Dad..." I interject, rather bluntly,
"Mark's a great kid.
He tries whatever I throw at him."
Mark looks up at me,
A bit unsure...

"When Mark understands, his eyes really light up!"
The other four teachers read my direction
and echo my comments.

"Yes, but he can do better!"
Dad interrupts.

"He is doing better,"
I quickly added,
Even though his progress at this point
Was difficult to measure.
"He's doing better every day.
He's interested...
He's pleasant...
He's cooperative...
He's going to be okay."
Now, I was the one who spoke unsurely.
Frankly, I was gambling.

The gamble paid off.
Mark did begin to do better.
He did begin to show interest.
He did begin to try.
He was cooperative.

Which left me with one question for dad:

"Ycanchube in Mark's corner?
You might produce a winner!"

1...2...3...Listening!

How many times
Have I told my kids,
"When you hear me say,
1...2...3...listening,
You need to use your best listening skills...
Or you'll miss something important!"
I always make sure they know what good listening
Looks like
And
Sounds like.
They respond well to the signal.

But,
Do I?
Do I take time to be sensitive
To those subtle signals...
Those words...
Looks...
Events...
Memories...
Which, if ignored,
Will signal the passage of something important to me?
Am I so busy teaching,
That I miss opportunities for learning?

This question has concerned me...
Pushed me...
Driven me...
To force myself to take time,
Each day,
To listen...
Listen and reflect on the meaning of what I am "hearing,"
Listening has become an irresistable urge...
An urge I cannot ignore.
Some days, I like what I hear:
A lesson well-taught...
A child turned on to learning...
A learner's need met...
All pleasant sounds to my "teacher-ear."

But,
Many days,
My reflections aren't pleasant.
Those are, perhaps,
The most valuable days of all.
For the failures...
The missed opportunities...
The forever lost teachable moments,
Are my doorway to personal growth...
If I am listening.

Fire Drill

May 9th.
Friday.
9:45 a.m.
FIRE DRILL!
No big deal for most of us,
But for James,
Oh, my!

Autistic.
Afraid of loud noises.
Allergic to any change in routine.
Fire drills are catastrophic!

Unless...
Of course...
He can find me and my wheelchair.
I tote him out of the building,
And back in,
On the back of my chair...
I guess you might say, "paraplegic piggyback!"
He has so much fun,
He forgets to be afraid.

Today,
He sent me a personalized,
Computerized message
He recorded on his laptop.
I guess he was using his technology
To thank me for using my technology
For making both our lives a little richer.

I'm sharing that message with you:

THANK YOU MR. PUCKIT FOR WHAT YOU
DID ON MAY 9, 1997 JAMES WILLIAMSON.

Biography of an Urban Textbook

In sorting through some old textbooks this afternoon,
I was drawn to the inside front cover
of book number 714368:
Human Heritage. Coronado, 1985.
I suppose all texts, everywhere,
Have the black box inside the front cover,
Where, year after year,
We write the names of the new group of students
on our enrollment lists.

I always wonder what kind of students they will be.
Will they be diligent,
Hard working,
Achieving?
Will they be one of those real challenges that
push us to our limit,
(And sometimes beyond)?
I've never been able to predict,
As I write those names in that little black box.
But, I continue to try,
Year after year.

As I looked at book number 714368,
I couldn't help pausing to consider the,
Now former, students whose names appeared there:

Maggie Mitchell	1987-1988	New
Eric Martin	1988-1989	Good
Tigist Griggs	1989-1990	Good
Donald Cooper	1990-1991	Poor
Lindsay Million	1991-1992	Badly Worn

I was amazed that I had been able to keep up
with those children,
Now young adults.

As seventh graders,
They all had promise...
Some more than others.

Maggie,
A superb student...
Far too mature for her years.
Married now.
Teaching in Tennessee.

Eric,
A learning-disabled student,
Wonderful boy...
A real gentleman.
Terribly dyslexic,
Struggled in high school.
Played college basketball,
Till he couldn't keep up academically.
Led his junior college team to a national championship.
His father and I always sat together at games
to cheer him on.
Working now.
Doing well.

Tigist,
A real sweetheart.
Polite.
Smart.
Quiet.
The world's biggest, brownest, trusting eyes.
Found along the roadside.
Murdered at age 19.
Case not solved.
I still haven't gotten over that one.
Tigist,
I won't forget you.

Donald,
Good old Donald.
Struggled in school.....some days,

Gave up.....most days,
Did well.....a few days.
The kids called him "Chewy".
I took Donald clothes shopping for Christmas that year,
Dad was out of work.
Still comes back to visit me
Several times a year.
Always gives me a big hug.
Don,
I really look forward to those hugs!

Lindsay,
What can I say?
You've made me so proud!
Governor's Scholar.
Full scholarship to the the school of your choice.
Go for it Lindsay,
Sky's the limit!

As I looked at those names,
And years again,
It was hard to realize how time had flown by.
It doesn't seem possible.

I couldn't force myself to write
CONDEMNED
In that old book.
Number 714368 was too much a part of me.
I slipped it from the stack
And laid on a table in my office.

I didn't open any other copies of the text.
I knew I wouldn't have adequate storage space.

I boxed them up,
Set them out for pick-up,
And said a silent prayer
For the names I couldn't bear to read.

Connections

Why is it that some kids
Have the unpretentious ability to melt the teacher's heart?
We've all had them...
I know we have!

They hang behind
After class...
After school...
In the lunch line...
For no particular reason.
They just want to talk...
To tell...
To ask...
To share a totally unimportant bit of information.

There are only one or two
Each year,
But,
They are always there.

They connect.
For some inexplicable reason
There is a link
Between the teacher
And
That special student.

Something essentially
Human...
Basic...
Elemental...
Essential.

Something not based on common background,
Or
Common interests,
Or
Common goals.
A sort of unconditional,
Unlikely
Friendship
Between
The old and the young,
Between
The past and the future,
In which each acknowledges and validates the other.

Those one or two each year
Are the ones who remain...
Who hang behind,
As years go on.
Remaining in your thoughts...
Returning to visit...
Writing from college...
Bringing their children to meet you...
Reminding you how old you are getting....
But
Through shared memory,
Through that inexplicable connection,
Helping you stay young.

It is,
I think,
In those one or two special kids,
Each year,
That the teacher finds
Immortality.

Does It Last a Lifetime?

I wrestle each day with a question
I have not yet been able to answer.
Each year I teach,
The question becomes more compelling,
The answer,
More elusive.

What are my students really learning?
What should they be learning?
What am I,
The man behind the desk,
Actually teaching them?
Is it enough?
Will it last a lifetime?

The only answer I have been given
Remains nebulous.
More in the realm of memory than fact.
I asked myself,
What do I remember from my 12th year?
What did I learn at 12 that has lasted a lifetime?

My responses surprise me.
I don't remember what we studied in science.
I couldn't tell you what we read in English.
I can't recall particular facts from geography class.
Math is still somewhat of a mystery.

But, what I truly learned,
I truly remember.

I remember feeling different...
Painfully different.
Having had polio,
Wearing leg braces,

Not wearing all the right styles....
Being different is hard.
Especially when you are 12.

Being different doesn't matter anymore.

What does matter,
And, I suppose,
Has always mattered,
Are the attitudes and values I saw modeled
When I was 12.

Mrs. Maurer...   The inexplicable pride of tackling a
difficult task successfuly.
Mr. Kane...   The sheer pleasure of exploring,
digging, probing into any topic
that interests you.
Mrs. Haan...   The absolute wonder of creativity,
whether in art or in teaching.
Mr. Collins...   The value of competition and working
together as a team.

And... perhaps...
Most memorable of all,,,
Mrs. Montgomery.

Mrs. Pat Montgomery... genuine, transparent
humanity... with no shame in tears... healing with
laughter... and the belief that truth is at the core of
the human spirit...

Mrs. Montgomery made me feel special...
That's what made being different no longer matter.

These are the lessons which have lasted a lifetime.

I pray, someday, I will be someone's Mrs. Montgomery.

High School Graduation

I attended a high school graduation this weekend,
Invited by a former student.
Sure I'd taught many of the graduates,
I watched the procession,
Scanning for familiar faces;
Faces I had spent three years of my life with.
But,
Much to my disappointment,
No recognition came.

These were strangers;
These almost-adults,
Walking triumphantly down the crowded aisle.

These were strangers;
These young men with beards and strong hands.

These were strangers;
These young women so well-poised,
Walking confidently in high heels.

I was there,
So I stayed,
Even though I knew no one.
I sat through the introductions...
The speeches...
The high school administrators proclaiming
their own greatness in producing
such unparalleled scholars.
Finally,
The awarding of diplomas.
Name after name.
Row upon row.
Then, I heard...
"Staceena Brummett...Honors Student...Scholarship Recipient..."
I couldn't believe it.

"Josh Greenwell... National Merit Scholarship Finalist...."

Another shock.

"Josh McCracken... National Merit Scholarship Semi-Finalist...."
Ah Ha!

These were not strangers!
But butterflies I had taught in the caterpillar phase.
Metamorphosis had, momentarily, confused me!

These were my students...
But in a new, and improved form.
No longer all feet,
Big ears,
No confidence,
Self-conscious.

No longer awkward,
Silly,
Over-reacting,
Almost-teens.

These were real people.
People who had achieved,
People who were on their way to a stage...
Instead of on their way through a stage.

"I need to remember this."
I thought.
"It might make the
He said/she said episodes,
The cracking voices,
The overdone makeup...
The slang books...
The notes....
Less significant."

"Remember this,"
I told myself,
"And attend a graduation every year,
In case you forget!"

Pliking

When I was a child,
We lived out in the country.
Few neighbors...
Few toys....
Just us.

Mother taught us the art of "Pliking":
The uninhibited ability to
"Play like..."
To pretend...
To exercise our imaginations.
How I have learned to appreciate those days.

One reason I love teaching pre-adolescents
Is because they haven't forgotten how to plike.

Oh,
At first they protest
When you announce that
"Today we are pliking!"
But,
Soon,
The announcement is soon followed by.....
"What are we going to plike, Mr. P.?"

Some days
We plike we can't write
and all communication must be oral.

Some days
We plike we can't speak and
all communication must be written.

Some days we plike we're in the Middle Ages;

Some days Ancient Greece.

Some days
We even plike our frown muscles don't work
Or
The words *don't* and *can't* don't exist in our language.

Not long ago
Our principal visited our classroom on a "pliking" day.
She was totally lost!
She didn't have a clue!

One of the kids called her over
And
Gently diagnosed the problem.

"Mrs. Miller,"
She whispered,
"Don't feel too bad.......
You just forgot how to plike when you grew up!"

Lord,
Keep fresh in us "grown-ups"
The joy of "Pliking."

Year's End

How do you say "Thank You" for a year of a child's life?
The learning...
The growing...
The laughing...
The grieving?
The time when the class becomes a family;
A family to support,
Encourage,
Comfort.
The closeness that the loss of a member brings.

How do you thank parents
for their support and involvement?
How do you thank peer tutors for the life they have shared?
How do you thank our very special students
For simply being themselves?

The only way to express the gratitude we feel...
Is simply to say,
"Thank you".....
And work to become the kind of person your students think
you already are.